Podcast 101:

Simple Steps to Create Your Own Podcast, Build Relationships and Grow Your Business

By

Paul G. Brodie

Podcast 101: Simple Steps to Create Your Own Podcast, Build Relationships and Grow Your Business

Published in the United States by BCG Publishing, 2019.

Disclaimer

The following viewpoints in this book are those of Paul Brodie. These views are based on his personal experience over the past forty-three years on the planet Earth, especially while living in the great state of Texas.

The intention of this book is to share his story about starting a podcast and what has worked for *him* through this journey.

All attempts have been made to verify the information provided by this publication. Neither the author nor the publisher assumes any responsibility for errors, omissions, or contrary interpretations of the subject matter herein.

This book is for entertainment purposes only. The views expressed are those of the author alone and should not be taken as expert instruction or commands. The reader is responsible for his or her future action. This book makes no guarantees of future success. However, by following the steps that are listed in this book the odds of starting your own podcast and growing your business have a much higher probability.

Neither the author nor the publisher assumes any responsibility or liability on the behalf of the purchaser or reader of these materials.

The views expressed are based on his personal experiences within the corporate world, education, and everyday life.

This book is dedicated to my mom, Barbara "Mama" Brodie. Without her support and motivation (and incredible cooking) I would literally not be here today.

I am also dedicating this book to every client that I have had the privilege to help grow their business through getting a book published or with starting a podcast. You have all gone above and beyond chasing your dreams and I am proud to be able to help in your journey.

Table of Contents

Invitation Join Our Get Published Business Book

Are you looking to Get Published with a proven system that works?

If you are looking to promote your business or just want to check off being a published author on the bucket list, this business book is for you.

Entrepreneurs and business owners, the benefits of writing and publishing a book is an ideal way to grow your business in addition to having a podcast. Publishing a book will give you instant authority in your specific area of expertise.

Begin your Author Journey Today:

- **Getting Started:** The Get Published Business Book will be a collection of people like you sharing your inspiration and motivation with others. Every author will receive your own chapter for a 500-750 word submission, along with the opportunity to include your personal contact information and website.
- **Instant Credibility:** Joining this collaboration will guarantee you instant Bestseller status and the rest of the work will be taken care of. Our team will handle the editing, formatting, the book

cover creation, marketing, etc. Everything will be done for you.

- **The Investment:** So how do you get in on this awesome opportunity? Easy payment options! 1 payment of $197 or 3 payments of $97 to gain instant credibility as a published bestselling author and be part of something bigger

Go to GetPublishedSystem.com to get more information about our Get Published Business Book

Foreword by Billy J. Atwell

I first met Paul when he was a guest on my podcast, **Unshakable Self-Confidence**. And as with most of my guests, I had a lengthy post-interview conversation with him. It was during that conversation that Paul and I started to discuss the possibility of me writing a book about everything I had learned about the nature of fear and developing self-confidence, and how to go about making that book a reality.

Cut to a few months later…I am deep in the process of writing my book, with Paul guiding through each step of that journey, as well as helping me to clearly see through the confusion and doubts that comes with the "newness" of any venture. Thanks to Paul, my book became a #1 bestseller in two weeks after being published and remained so for 7 months. It continues to be a bestseller to this day.

I don't have many friends. Not because I cannot make friends, or that I am some horrid and retched human-being that nobody can stand to be around. I don't have many friends by choice. As Brené Brown says, "people need to earn the marbles to put into the trust jar," and I have found that most people are more interested in "taking" marbles out of the jar instead of "putting" them in. To the point, Paul is one of those individuals who has earned my trust, and as such, we have developed a mutual admiration for one another, giving advice freely in order to help the other in our separate business ventures.

It was during one of those conversations that I mentioned to Paul that he needed a podcast of his own. He asked if I would show him the ropes. I said yes. In a fashion true to Paul, he created a book, this book, to help others clearly navigate through the vague and often hazy perceptions and misconceptions (and yes, be honest, difficult and frustrating situations) of what it takes to create a podcast.

Since you bought this book in faith, let me help you to solidify that faith in your decision.

Paul is a genuinely humble and honest human-being. His true nature is a giving one, directed in helping anyone achieve their goals. I can also tell you that Paul is not what I would call a "surface-skimmer" when it comes to researching and figuring out workable systems, like most of the so-called "gurus" out there; he is a "deep-diver!"

My advice to you is to proceed forward, take notes, get the resources offered and most importantly, put into action the steps Paul tells you to take. If you do, before you know it, your dream of being a podcaster will go from just being a dream, and manifest into a reality.

My very best to you on this journey!

Be well and peaceful,

Billy J. Atwell
Founder, *Unshakable Self-Confidence*

Podcast Invitation

I want to invite you to check out our podcast.

It is called Get Published and is perfect for listeners who want to get great information about the author journey in a short period of time.

Each episode is fast paced where we ask our guests 5 questions about every step of the author journey, to help you with the writing, publishing and marketing of your book.

Give us 15 minutes and we will give you a great podcast.

Get Published has over 200 episodes available and is hosted by 13-time bestselling author, coach, and book publisher, Paul G. Brodie.

Go to GetPublishedPodcast.com to listen to the Get Published Podcast

Introduction

Welcome to my 14th book. This is not your typical how to book. It is for people who want to know how to start a podcast quickly and in the most efficient manner possible. This book is for people who want to start a podcast with a proven system that works. If you want to use your podcast to build relationships and grow your business, then this book is for you. Having your own podcast is one of the best ways to establish authority and be able to sell your services to the warmest leads possible.

Many of the costs involved with starting and maintaining your podcast are tax deductible, but always check with your accountant first.

Have you always wanted to have your own podcast? Do you find it difficult to know where to start? Has a family member or friend said that you should have your own show?

I want to tell you that every person has a podcast in them and this book will help you start a podcast with a proven system that works. One of the biggest challenges about having your own podcast is getting started. We all struggle with sharing ourselves with the world and having your own show can appear scary. I can assure you that if I can build my own podcast with over 200 episodes in the past year, then you can as well. This is what we will cover in get Podcast 101:

Chapter 1: Everyone Should Have a Podcast

Chapter 2: How to Run your Podcast Like a Business

Chapter 3: Choosing Your Podcast Title and Description and Why Both are Critical in the Success of Your Podcast

Chapter 4: Creating the Format for Your Podcast

Chapter 5: Designing Your Podcast Cover

Chapter 6: Finding the Right Equipment

Chapter 7: Choosing the Best Software

Chapter 8: Using the Best Hosting Service

Chapter 9: Creating an Intro and Outro

Chapter 10: Sponsors for Your Podcast

Chapter 11: The Process on Recording, Editing, and Uploading Your Podcast

Chapter 12: Getting Your Podcast on iTunes, Google Play, and Spotify

Chapter 13: How to Find Guests for Your Podcast

Chapter 14: Guiding Your Guest Through the Podcast Process

Chapter 15: Post Interview Process with Your Guest

Chapter 16: Marketing Your Podcast

Chapter 17: Making Revenue on the Back-End

Chapter 18: Summary: Podcast 101

I hope this book helps in your journey to start your own podcast. My philosophy in anything I do in life, whether it's teaching, giving motivational seminars, and writing and coaching, is to have the power of one. The power of one is my goal to help at least one person. I hope that person is you.

Free Book

I would like to offer you the digital version of Get Published. The brand-new second edition of Get Published will only be available on the website for a limited time. Enjoy!

Go to GetPublishedSystem.com to download your free copy of Get Published

Chapter 1

Everyone Should Have a Podcast

"You have something special inside you. Something you know. Something you do. Something you can teach. You are already an expert." Robert Kiyosaki

Have you always wanted to start a podcast? Do you find it difficult to know where to start?

Would you like someone to introduce you as a podcast host? Could you imagine if that happened to you? Are you ready to get started in your podcasting journey?

I started this chapter with multiple questions because I want to tell you that everyone has a podcast in them. This book will help you start a podcast with a proven system that works. One of the biggest challenges is getting your podcast started.

Having your own podcast can change your life. It gives you instant credibility and positions you as an expert in your area of expertise.

That is why starting a podcast is critical to every business owner who wants to grow his or her business. I help my clients in the United States, United Kingdom, Canada, Australia, and New Zealand not only with getting their books published, but also by helping many of them to start their own podcast.

In 2018, I joined both the Arlington Chamber of Commerce and the Arlington Sunrise Rotary Club, so I could give back and connect with local businesses. Service to others is something that I live by, as my personal motto is Veritas et Utilitas, which translates roughly to truth and service. Those are also the two core values of my business.

I view truth as being completely honest and direct with my clients. This also includes complete transparency as I walk them through the entire process including timelines.

When I was introduced to both the Chamber and Rotary, I was introduced as a 13-time bestselling author. It immediately got the attention of those in the room and I had multiple people approach me to ask about my business, as well as how I could help them write a book. The root word of authority is author and gives you both instant credibility and a warm introduction to people you want to meet.

My response to every person who approached me was that everyone has a book in them. These days I also encourage them to start their own podcast in addition to having their own book.

My company expanded over the past year and now offers our Book Publishing Implementation Program, One-On-One Executive Coaching, Done For You Book

Publishing Service, Done For You Book Launch Marketing Service, Executive Ghostwriting for Business Owners and Executives who want to share their story, and our Done For You Podcast Production Services.

I started the Get Published Podcast in June 2018 and generated over five figures in business through relationships with guests for that year. We are projected to go over six figures in 2019 from business with podcast guests. In January 2019, we have already made significant progress towards that goal due to the record breaking business we completed. Most of the revenue was due to podcast guests and referrals from those guests. In this book I am going to show you how you can also utilize your podcast to grow your own business by building relationships and not being salesy.

The reason I bring up my services is because I feel that starting a podcast is potentially life-changing to both you and your business. Starting your podcast correctly and with a proven system that works is key to the success of your book. I learned from the great Russell Brunson (Founder of Click Funnels) in his Expert Secrets book, that we have a moral obligation to share our message because it is life changing and can help others. I have seen how my client's lives have changed and I want to help you do the same.

The main things to know about starting a podcast is that everyone has a show in them and that you must run your podcast like a business. In the next chapter, that is exactly what I am going to show you.

Chapter 2

Running Your Podcast like a Business

"To each there comes in their lifetime a special moment when they are figuratively tapped on the shoulder and offered the chance to do a very special thing, unique to them and fitted to their talents. What a tragedy if that moment finds them unprepared or unqualified for that which could have been their finest hour." Sir. Winston Churchill

Would you like to use your podcast to grow your business? Now that you have decided to start a podcast you need to answer one critical question before you start. What do you want to get out of your show?

Do you want to grow your business with your podcast? Is creating the podcast something that you want to check off your bucket list? Do you want to sell a new service with the podcast? What services do you want to offer?

We all have one shot to make a first impression with our listeners and guests. With that shot, you must realize that your podcast is the key to growing your business and you must run it like a business and not a hobby.

Running your podcast like a business is critical to your future success and you must know what you want to get out of your podcast before getting started. Another question to answer is, how will your show help other people?

Is your podcast going to teach someone how to do something? My podcast helps people in their author journey. I have guests on the show from all over the world that talk about the author journey. This was something deeply personal to me because in 2011, I was close to 340 pounds, had multiple health issues to a point where my Doctor said I would be dead in five years if I didn't get my act together.

Over the next year, I lost 60 pounds and kept the weight off. What was the secret of my transformation? I chose to eat less and move more and wanted to share both the victories and setbacks with losing weight. In 2015, I wrote my first book, Eat Less and Move More. It completely changed my life when it became my first bestseller.

Podcast 101 is my 14th book since starting my own author journey. Like having your own book, you must focus on the back-end with selling services to monetize your podcast. Initially, I wrote my books to help people who were struggling with weight and to increase business for my speaking business. Then a funny thing happened that was completely unexpected…

Readers and fellow authors began contacting me and asked if I could help them get published. At the time, I published my third bestseller called Positivity Attracts. The book was launched around Thanksgiving 2015 and was my biggest success yet. Positivity Attracts combined with my two other books brought me the first of many four figure months in royalties. It also got the attention of many people who also wanted to get published with a proven system.

People often ask me if I went through a publishing course or had personal coaching when I started out. I always made it clear that I was self-taught. Everything I learned was the hard way and through many hours of research, trial and error, listening to author summits, podcasts, reading articles, and learning as much as possible about marketing.

I share this story because starting my own podcast also was a challenge. It was very similar to when I had to learn everything possible about publishing back in 2015.

Additionally, it is why I am a huge believer in either hiring a coach or utilizing a Done For You Podcast Service to help you as it will accelerate your journey to get your podcast started. Hiring a coach or service will help you get your podcast started much faster than doing it yourself because it will help you with focus, accountability, speed, and support. This is why I offer Done For You services with my company, in addition to coaching. I want to help my clients get started quickly with systems that are proven to work.

I was very fortunate that one of my publishing clients had a podcast. My client, Billy Atwell told me multiple times that I must start a podcast to share my knowledge with the world about getting published. He was instrumental in guiding me through the process and was the one who highly encouraged me to write this book as there aren't many helpful books about Podcasting. Regardless of who you choose to work with, get someone to help guide you through the process. There is a learning curve with having your own podcast. In this book, I will do my best to give you many of the tools to help in your own podcast journey.

As you have noticed with my story, having my own book and podcast was life changing. I am now able to help people get published and start their own podcast. Do you see how this can change your business?

Chapter 3

Choosing Your Podcast Title

Choosing your podcast title is critical to the success of your book. Have you decided on the name for your podcast? Do you feel that the podcast title stands out? When it comes to choosing a podcast title, you want to choose one that will be easy to search for.

I was a teacher for nine years and one of the greatest lessons I have learned is that we must make things as simple as possible. Don't make an overly complex or complicated title. You want something that is short, direct, and to the point.

My podcast, after much consideration, was going to be called The Get Published Podcast. My company branding (including my Get Published book) was all about helping people get published with a proven system.

Once you decide on your title, you will need a description for the show. Here is my podcast description: *Welcome to the Get Published Podcast, where we help authors get published with a proven system that works! Give us 15 minutes and we will give you a great podcast. Join 13-time bestselling author and publishing coach, Paul Brodie as he discusses with his guest, every step of the author journey, to help you with the writing, publishing and marketing of your book.*

I view the description like the subtitle of a book. You want to go into detail about the benefit the listener will get out of the show. Covering the outcome is critical in your description as you want to tell the listener what is in it for them.

Once you have the title and description of your podcast decided, then you need to figure out the format of your show.

Chapter 4

Creating the Format for Your Podcast

Now that you have created both your podcast title and description, it is time to figure out the format of your show. Do you want the show episodes to be short or long? Are you planning to ask the same questions on each episode?

One piece of advice I would like to give is to consider having a short show. The Get Published Podcast is typically 10-20 minutes per episode. I have found that most of my podcast listeners want episodes to be around 10-20 minutes as it is short, direct, and to the point. The attention spans of listeners tend to be shorter these days, so having a show that is short, direct, and can be binged listened to is a great fit with today's listeners.

Having a shorter show makes it easier to record and helps with both recording and producing multiple episodes of the show. In the first five months of the Get Published Podcast we were able to record over 200 episodes with minimal edits. We will cover the recording and producing parts about your podcast later in this book.

The next item to consider is if you want to ask the same questions on each show or create different questions for each show.

It is much easier to use the same questions on each show. You might think that might be a boring option, but it really is not. The key is to use the same 5 base questions and ask follow-up questions based on the guests' responses. It does take some practice, however, if the podcast is based on an area of your expertise, it will become easier once you get the show started and have recorded the first 10 episodes.

Chapter 5

Designing Your Podcast Cover

I want you to start thinking about your podcast cover. This is very similar to my philosophy with having a book cover created before you start writing a book. The main reason is inspiration. Even though you may not have everything ready for your podcast, I know that you have an idea for where you want to go. When I am helping my clients with their book covers, I always tell them to visualize the cover and what they want to see. From that point, I help them make that vision a reality. It is the same thing with your podcast cover.

Consider the following questions. What color do you want in the background of the podcast cover? What color do you want the podcast title text to be in? What image should you use for the podcast cover?

Having a great looking podcast cover for your show is one of the most important parts about having a successful podcast. Listeners do judge a show by its podcast cover (just like a book is judged by its cover) and you will want to have the best-looking podcast cover possible.

When you are deciding on your podcast cover, you want to look at several factors.

You want it to be eye-catching. It needs to grab the attention of the listener.

You also want to have great colors in the podcast cover. Orange has proven to do well as that color not only stands out, but also elicits a buying response in potential customers. Having a bold font in the podcast title is also important, as you want to have the actual title stand out.

The podcast show image needs to look great in the thumbnail view on iTunes, Libsyn, Google Play, etc. When you do a search of podcasts on those sites, you will see the results in list form. The podcast image will be in a much smaller format, otherwise known as a thumbnail view. Having a great looking cover with a clear and bold title will stand out, especially when competing with other podcasts for the listeners attention.

The podcast cover is your window dressing. Choosing the right podcast cover is critical to your podcast for both branding and to get the attention of the listener. Podcast cover designs can range in cost from five dollars to several hundred dollars.

In 2015, I wrote my first book and needed to find a book cover designer. I researched Fiverr extensively and found a freelancer who made book covers for a very inexpensive cost and had a great rating from customers.

In fact, she has thousands of ratings, so I figured I would give it a shot. I was not disappointed.

Everything on Fiverr is at least five dollars to start, but there are always extras. I chose the twenty-dollar option for my first three books, which included the five-dollar gig, an additional five dollars for a high-quality stock image, and ten dollars for the original PSD file and PDF. This was a great investment, so I could have the master copy in case I ever needed to make any changes.

In the request for my first book cover, I asked for a blue and black color scheme. Within four days, my designer delivered my first book cover and I loved it.

In 2017, I hired a new book cover designer and he is the main person I use for my books and for my client books. He made the cover for my podcast.

I would suggest searching on Fiverr and Upwork for book cover designers. A good book cover designer can also create images for podcast covers. Send them a message and tell them you're looking for a cover design for your podcast and tell them the size you will need. For podcast covers, you need to have an image that is either a jpg or png file, the size of the podcast cover needs to be 1400 by 1400 pixels and 300 dpi. All you need to do is tell the designer that information and they will be able to make you a podcast show image. Below is the podcast cover my book cover designer made for my Get Published Podcast.

Having a great looking podcast cover image that grabs the attention of the reader is critical. Before we wrap up this chapter, I want to share how you can create a rough mockup of your podcast cover image. I am a terrible artist and cannot draw at all. However, I can do some basic design concepts. If I can create a rough mockup of a podcast cover, then anyone can.

When I think of a podcast cover image, I do searches on google. I find images that I feel will fit the cover and then figure out the placement of where I want the title, background, and image design. You always want your title to be visible with placement on the middle or top part of the podcast cover.

When creating a podcast cover, you want to be able to see it clearly in both a regular and thumbnail view. Once you have a general idea of what you want then you can send the information to your cover designer and make clear what you want in the cover design.

One thing I will do is create a mock design in Microsoft Word. I will create the podcast title with the font and color that I want. Below the font and color will be the design image that I want in the cover. Once everything is done, I will send it to my cover designer.

By using that process, you should be able to come up with a great podcast cover design. I also recommend downloading podcast images that you like that you feel stand out. Create a folder on your computer and save every podcast image that you like in that file. You will have a great library of images to help you find inspiration for your podcast design.

Chapter 6

Equipment for Your Podcast

Over the next two chapters I am going to cover both the equipment and software that I recommend that you use for your podcast. The equipment is the same that I use for the Get Published Podcast. If you have a laptop that was bought in the past two years, then you will not need a new laptop or desktop computer. I have used my Lenovo laptop for the Get Published Podcast and have not had any problems.

The first piece of equipment to buy is a great microphone. When I started recording my own audiobooks, I bought a condenser microphone called the Blue Snowball ICE Condenser Microphone and a pop filter from Amazon. The cost was around $56.00 for both. I used that mic to record seven of my audiobooks.

In 2017, I bought a new microphone and it is the one that I highly recommend that you buy for your podcast. It is the ATR 2100-USB Cardioid Dynamic Microphone. Many authors use this mic to record audiobooks and many podcast hosts use the mic for their podcasts. You can buy the ATR 2100 on Amazon for around sixty-five dollars.

Another option is to buy a microphone suspension mic clip adjustable boom studio scissor arm stand. You can find it on Amazon for around twelve dollars. Once you receive the stand all you need to do is use the adjustable mount to mount it to your desk. Having the stand installed will make the set-up process easy and will literally take you a few short minutes to set up for recording.

The next piece of equipment is the most important after the microphone. It is the pre-amp. The pre-amp is critical to record the audio on both your end and with recording the audio of the guest. I use the Focusrite Scarlett 6i6 pre-amp. Originally, I bought the Focusrite Scarlett Solo and the Scarlett Solo would not record the audio of my guest, it only recorded my voice. I contacted tech support at Focusrite and they told me the Scarlett Solo would not record the audio of my guest and that I need to buy the Scarlett 6i6. Once I bought the Scarlett 6i6 everything worked great. You will also need to buy an additional cable for the pre-amp to connect the audio on the amp by connecting the line output to the line input on the back of the pre-amp. The cable is only five dollars. I bought the Hosa CSS-103 1/4-inch TRS to 1/4-inch TRS Balanced Interconnect Cable, 3 feet. All you need to do is type that information in the search bar on Amazon and you will be taken to that exact cable.

I will cover the software portion with the Focusrite Scarlett 6i6 in the next chapter. Best part is that you will be able to contact Focusrite as they will help set up your software through their tech support and they will be able to set up your software for you though their screen share abilities to ensure that everything works correctly.

You will also need to buy a headset for the podcast. By having the headset, you will ensure that you do not have echo nor audio interference. You can use a regular headset or ear buds that you would use for music or you can buy a professional headset. I used a headset that I already used for music and bought an adapter, so I could connect it to the Focusrite pre-amp. The adapter is two dollars and can be bought on Amazon or at an electronic store like Fry's. All you need to do is type in 6.35 mm Male to 3.5 mm Female Stereo Adapter Headphone. You will see lots of choices on Amazon. If you go to an electronics store, then tell them you are looking for a 6.35 mm Male to 3.5 mm Female Stereo Adapter so you can connect your headphones to the pre-amp.

That will be all the equipment that is needed. I do highly recommend the equipment mentioned. It is exactly what I use for the Get Published Podcast.

Chapter 7

Software for Your Podcast

Once you have the right equipment for your podcast, it is time for you to choose the software for your show. The first decision is which software to use to record your podcast. After much consideration, I chose Adobe Audition. It costs twenty dollars a month, is user friendly, and is easy to use. I have used Adobe Audition to record over two hundred episodes of the Get Published Podcast. I love using it!

The Focusrite Scarlett 6i6 pre-amp includes the Focusrite Control Software, which is excellent. As I mentioned in chapter 6, the software that is included with the amp can be installed easily and the Focusrite tech support team can help you with the setup of the mixer and ensure the software is working correctly. The best part is that the support is complimentary with purchase and they do great work.

If you do not want to spend twenty dollars a month, then you can download Audacity. It is a free program that I have used to record many of my audiobooks and you could use that option for your podcast. Audacity can be downloaded on https://www.audacityteam.org if you want to download the program. If you are a mac user, then you can use Garage Band, which is already available on your mac computer.

Another software program you will need is the ID3 Editor. The software program lets you add all the information from each podcast episode into the MP3 File of each podcast episode once you have produced and edited the episode. The program also lets you add the podcast cover artwork for each episode. The ID3 Editor costs $15.00 and can be purchased on www.pa-software.com if you want to download it.

You will also want to consider investing in a software player that will play episodes of your podcast. I use the Smart Podcast Player. I installed the Smart Podcast Player on the front page of my website where people who visit my site can listen to every episode of the podcast. It costs twelve dollars per month and is a great program so that listeners can easily access the podcast directly on your website.

Go to https://smartpodcastplayer.com to get more information about the Smart Podcast Player.

I recommend using Skype for your podcast interviews. Most potential guests have used Skype before or are at least familiar with it. Even if the guest does not use Skype, you can still use Skype to call their phone for the podcast interview. You can buy subscriptions for a specific country to save money when calling phone numbers through Skype. The subscription for unlimited calling in the United States is around three dollars a month. All calls across the world that are done from one Skype account to another Skype account is free. It only costs money when you are calling a phone number.

Zoom is another option, but it is not always user friendly. My decision to use Skype was based on simplicity for both me and for our guests as you want to make the process as easy as possible.

In the next chapter we will cover hosting options for your podcast.

Chapter 8

Podcast Hosting

Throughout this book, I am covering what I have used for my podcast. I do not have any affiliate links or special arrangements with anyone. I am wanting to share what has worked well for me and most importantly will help you and reduce the learning curve.

My recommendation is to use Libsyn (Liberated Syndication) to host your podcast. Go to https://www.libsyn.com to get more information. Their monthly billing starts at five dollars a month and goes up to seventy-five dollars per month. If you are only recording a few episodes per month then I would recommend the Libsyn Classic 250 service, which costs fifteen dollars per month.

The Get Published Podcast started with releasing one episode a week back in June 2018. By Mid-August, we expanded the podcast to five new releases per week. In October, we continued to release five new episodes each week, and did an additional upload of twenty-five episodes at the end of the month due to the amount of shows we recorded. We have done the same thing from November, December, and January with uploading an additional thirty episodes at the end of each month and we are now finally caught up on our shows.

Currently we use the Libsyn Advanced 800 plan that includes an extra 200 MB and costs fifty dollars a month. It was well worth it as I have one gig of data each month and it ensures that I can release up to fifty new episodes per month with their hosting service.

Chapter 9

Creating an Intro and Outro

Once you get comfortable with Adobe Audition you will need to start thinking about your intro and outro. You can record it yourself or you can hire someone to record it for you. Fiverr and Upwork both have many different freelancers who will record both an intro and outro for a fee.

Personally, I would recommend that you record the intro and outro yourself. The main reason is because it will build a better connection between you and the listener. It is also why I record my own audiobooks. I want to connect with the reader. By recording it yourself, the listener gets familiar with your voice. This is especially crucial if you choose to add a "call to action" in the intro. A call to action is a specific prompt designed to illicit an immediate response or sale from your audience, like "sign up now".

After researching many different podcasters once I started my show, I learned that one of the biggest mistakes I made was not having a call to action in the intro. You always want to offer something to the audience, especially as they connect with you through your many episodes of content that you will be releasing.

I learned this the hard way. I didn't offer a call to action until after thirty episodes of my own podcast. An intro needs to be around 15-30 seconds and be direct and to the point.

This is my podcast intro: *"Welcome to the Get Published Podcast, sponsored by Brodie Consulting Group. To get more information about our coaching, publishing, executive ghostwriting, and podcast production services go to* www.GetPublishedPodcast.com.*"*

I also have music as part of the intro as you want to give it both a professional presentation and get the listener ready for your show. You can purchase music at www.AudioJungle.net with prices ranging from few dollars to more than one hundred dollars. The music that I chose cost me twenty dollars including fees.

My outro also includes the music I purchased and the following: *"Thanks again for joining us today. To learn more about how you can be featured in our brand new Get Published Business Book, go to*

www.GetPublishedPodcast.com.*"*

Intros and outros are great because you can make the podcast episode about your guest, without making it sound like you are constantly pitching your services. Having calls to action on both the intro and outro is a great way to have prospective clients reach out to you.

Paul Brodie

Chapter 10

Sponsors for Your Podcast

In chapter 9, I touched on the importance of having both an intro and outro. Both can be used to promote your services. I have had many conversations with friends who have their own podcasts and they gave me one main piece of advice.

That one main piece of advice was to not seek sponsorships. Instead, promote your own services by having your company as the sponsor of the podcast. Why promote someone else's business when you can promote your own services?

Therefore, having your own podcast is critical for your business and for lead generation. If you have this wonderful platform of podcasting in front of you then you should be promoting your own services as the main sponsor. The best part is that it is not being too pushy because you can use the intro and outro for the promotion, then just get on the with show when you start recording.

However, if you do want sponsorships, then you have options. I would recommend checking out the sponsorship opportunities that Libsyn offers. They have several advertising programs. To qualify, you must average at least 20,000 downloads a month. For more information go to https://four.libsyn.com/monetizing.

You can also approach sponsors yourself. All you need to do is research companies that you feel would be a good fit and go to their website. Find the main points of contact and send them an email. In the email, you want to tell them about your podcast and why it would benefit their business to sponsor your show. You will want to tell them about your audience and how many downloads your show gets.

If they are interested, send a second email with your offer and include when their company would be promoted during the show (intro, outro). One other area that you would promote the sponsor is called the midroll. The midroll is usually in the middle of the podcast episode and is essentially a commercial for the sponsor. Personally, I am not a fan of midrolls as I feel it detracts from the show. However, it is an option if you want to go in that direction.

As your podcast builds over time, you will most likely have sponsors that will reach out to you about sponsoring the show. Even though my podcast is only a few months old, sponsorship opportunities have presented themselves. However, I have chosen to not take on sponsorships at this time.

My dad gave me great advice a few years ago. He said the greatest investment we can make is not in stocks and bonds, it is investing in our own business. My dad has been a successful businessman in many industries and his advice always stuck with me. Due to that advice, I feel the best sponsorship opportunities should be to promote our own service and products.

My company offers coaching, book publishing, book launch marketing, executive ghostwriting, and podcast production services. Those services range from $1,000-$30,000. I would be foolish to not offer calls to action to grow my own business during the intro and outro of the podcast.

It does work! We have added significant business since starting the podcast. The decision to have my own company as the sponsor has proven to be the correct one.

Chapter 11

Recording, Editing, and Uploading Your Podcast

Libsyn has a simple to follow process to create your account. To help you with this process, I have created a quick video to walk you through the process at https://www.brodieedu.com/podcast101help

Now that you have your equipment and software, it is time to cover the recording, and editing process. I am going to show you exactly how to easily record your podcast.

I record my show in one take. The intro and outro are already recorded, so all I am doing is recording the main episode. I will be using Adobe Audition for this example. To make this as smooth as possible, I have recorded a quick video to walk you through the process at https://www.brodieedu.com/podcast101help

Once the podcast is recorded, then you need to mix the episode with the intro, outro, and reduce noise and use what is called a de-esser. Here is a quick video that will walk you through the process at

https://www.brodieedu.com/podcast101help

Now that you have mixed your episode, it is time to tag your episode with ID3. This includes adding your podcast cover, information about both the show and specific episode description, copyright information, website link. Here is a quick video that will walk you through the process at

https://www.brodieedu.com/podcast101help

Everything is now ready to go, and it is time to upload your podcast episode to Libsyn. The process includes uploading your show, adding the podcast title and description for iTunes, and publishing the show. Here is a quick video that will walk you through the process at
https://www.brodieedu.com/podcast101help

With the videos I have provided for you, it is a much easier option to show those how to videos as you need to visually see the process. There is nothing that is necessarily difficult about getting your show recorded, edited, and uploaded. The steps can be tedious and was why I specifically made walkthrough videos to help you through this process.

Chapter 12

Getting Your Podcast on iTunes, Google Play, and Spotify

By the time you have made it through chapter 11, you already have a few podcast episodes uploaded and are ready to share them with the world. Now it is time to get your podcast on iTunes, Google Play, Spotify, and Sound Cloud.

The best part is that you will only have to set it up once. Once it is set up, you will be able to go into the destinations tab in Libsyn and each podcast episode will be automatically published once you upload it on Libsyn.

Here is a walk-through video I made to help you set everything set up at
https://www.brodieedu.com/podcast101help

Chapter 13

Finding Guests for Your Podcast

One of the most important parts about your podcast is finding guests to be on your show. We started our own system to recruit guests on the show and we utilize one main source and that is LinkedIn. My team does searches for guests in five countries: United States, Canada, England, Australia, and New Zealand.

I chose those countries because I already help clients in those locations and I knew that would be a great base for the show's audience. We created a plan to reach out to those authors and invite them on the show. Out of the 200 plus episodes we have recorded, over 90 percent of our guests were from LinkedIn.

In the initial connection request, I include the following information: "Hey (First Name), Would love to connect and have you on my Get Published Podcast. I interview guests who are writing a book or have published a book. If you are interested, you can click a time to book at https://calendly.com/pbrodie/15min Cheers, Paul"

Once they accept the connection, they can go to Calendly and set up their interview. I do interviews in four 30 min time blocks Monday through Thursday, in the afternoon. In January, I scaled that down to four 30-

minute time blocks from Tuesday through Thursday as we now have plenty of podcast episodes.

You have probably noticed the link shows a time of 15 minutes. I like to emphasize that most of my episodes are around fifteen minutes. It helps with encouraging our potential guests to book a time since it is short and direct. With the 30 min block, I can build rapport prior to the show recording and also again by talking with the guest after the show to discuss possible next steps.

One thing I want to emphasize is to not be salesy on both your show and with your guest. The #1 thing you want to accomplish with your podcast is building not only an audience, but also a closer relationship with your listener and guest. People do business with those who they know, like, and trust. Having your podcast gives you the opportunity to do all three.

My approach is very simple with my guests as we wrap up the show. Once the show is recorded, I ask them about their next book. If they do have an upcoming book, I ask for their permission to send them more information about our services and how we help authors in their journey. I make it crystal clear that our company is not salesy and that we have a personalized and holistic approach with our clients. Over 95 percent of my guests always say yes to the request. Through this process, we have brought on multiple guests as clients and you do not have to be salesy to do so.

Paul Brodie

Chapter 14

Guiding Your Guest Through the Process

One of the most important parts about your podcast is your show up percentage. The show up percentage is the percentage of people who sign up for the podcast interview and actually show up. I have spoken to quite a few friends who are podcasters and they typically tell me their show up percentage is between 50-66%. My show up rate is over 80%.

I created a system that ensured that my guests show up. The first thing I do is make sure the Calendly link includes the name of the guest, email address, an option for their phone number or Skype ID, and the name of their book. This made research on my side much easier and gave me their contact information and the name of their book.

When the guest books a time, my team sends them an email (typically that day) with an interview confirmation and next steps. We will ask the guest to send us their picture, so we can add it to the infographic for when the podcast episode goes live. It also gives the guest some skin in the game since they know we will be using several promotional strategies and their picture. On the weekend prior to their interview, my team sends out a second podcast confirmation email. That email reminds the guest of their upcoming interview with the scheduled date and time for the podcast interview and we include the questions for the show including their intro.

The guest receives the Get Published Podcast Questions email on the weekend before their interview and through those first two emails, the guest has everything they need for the show. I also cover that we are recording the episode and that it is only audio. Having the interview as audio tends to make the show more relaxed since a lot of guests are not fans of video calls.

The other benefit is that I send the guest the questions before the interview, so they can prepare themselves on their own time. Many of my guests thank me for the questions in advance and the professional approach that we have.

Below are a couple examples of the infographic that we use to promote each episode. The infographics were created at www.canva.com

THE GET PUBLISHED PODCAST

HELPING AUTHORS GET PUBLISHED WITH A PROVEN SYSTEM THAT WORKS!

AVAILABLE NOW

EPISODE 143: PARIS CUTLER - CHOOSING THE BEST DATE TO LAUNCH YOUR BOOK

THE GET PUBLISHED PODCAST

HELPING AUTHORS GET PUBLISHED WITH A PROVEN SYSTEM THAT WORKS!

AVAILABLE NOW

EPISODE 166: NOBBY KLEINMAN - CONVERTING YOUR BOOK INTO A VIDEO

Chapter 15

Post Interview Process

Once the interview is done and the call has ended, it is time for the post interview process. If your guest has given you permission to send them information about your services, then send the services email the evening of the interview. You always want to get them the information as soon as possible.

I do recommend that you send the services email yourself instead of having your team send it. My team sends all of the other emails, but I always send the services email. This is due to wanting to create a closer and more personalized bond with the guest.

The period from the recording of the interview to the podcast episode going live should be six to eight weeks at the most. Make sure you are clear with your guest when you wrap up the call that the episode should be available in six to eight weeks and that you (or a member of your team) will be sending them an update via email the day before the episode goes live.

This became an issue for me with having over 100 additional episodes that were recorded back in November 2018 that still were not available. We ended up having a two-month delay for our guests that I knew needed fixed. Fortunately, we did fix the lag and now only have a four to six-week period before their episode goes live.

Also, make sure to tell them what will happen on the date that it does go live. I always tell my guest they will receive an email when it goes live, and it will have the following three links. The first link is of the podcast episode that they can share on their social media and website. Second link takes them to our Get Published iTunes Page and I ask if they could please leave a review about the show as we would really appreciate their support. The third and final link is a quick video that shows them how to leave the review on iTunes in case they might not be familiar with the process. We have received many reviews from our guests through this method. At the end of the email, we ask if they have friends who would a potential fit for the show. We also welcome them to reply to the email with any questions and if there is anything else we can do to help in their author journey.

What I highly recommend is that you create a Google Doc and share it with your team. Create rows that list the following: episode number, date the show was recorded, date the show was released, first and last name, email/contact information, notes from communication with guest, last date of contact, name of the guest's book, the specific services email that we sent them (we have several different emails), and the podcast episode link for every guest.

Having a Google Doc is a great way to keep everything organized and helps with the follow up process and relationship building. Walking the guest through the post interview process is key to getting them to share the episode link once it goes live and to continue to stay in contact. One of the greatest lessons I have learned is that follow-up is key. Using this process and a Google Doc will help with taking care of your guest throughout the interview process.

Chapter 16

Marketing Your Podcast

The best way to market your podcast is to utilize your platform. When I launched the Get Published Podcast, it was in conjunction with the launch of my Get Published Book. I also promoted the podcast through my email list, social media on Facebook, LinkedIn, and Twitter. The other key was getting my guests to promote their episode when it went live.

One lesson I learned is that I should have offered graphics when starting the show. I am mentioning it now because we now offer graphics to our guests and it does increase the likelihood they will promote it on their platform. You can create graphics in Canva and even have a template made on Fiverr and Upwork. My amazing VP - Customer Relations made custom graphics for each guest. Not only did she make the new graphics, but she reached out to our previous guests and offered to make them for those guests as well. I shared several examples in the previous chapter of the infographics that we use for promotion.

The graphic can be the main image from your podcast cover and then you can add the guest's professional picture to feature them. It is a personalized approach and something that took me several months to identify.

I would also encourage you to friend your guests on Facebook. That way, when you do post the episode to social media, you can tag them in it. You will already be able to do that on LinkedIn and doing so on Facebook will increase the reach even more. Your guests will already most likely have a social media following on multiple platforms.

Another great way to build your audience is releasing multiple episodes each week. It is a lot of work getting started, but once you get into a rhythm then it becomes much easier. I would recommend recording ten episodes to get started and release the first three episodes at the same time. The first episode should be what is called episode 0 and should be an episode that introduces yourself to the audience and to tell them about your background and how the show will help them. Here is the link to my episode 0 at -

http://getpublishedpodcast.libsyn.com/paul-g-brodie-what-you-will-get-out-of-listening-to-get-published

Once you have started releasing episodes of your podcast, consider releasing a new episode on Monday, Wednesday, and Friday. Podcast listeners love to consume content and starting out with multiple episodes available weekly will help build your audience quickly.

Chapter 17

Making Revenue on the Back-End

Back-end products are going to be where you make the most revenue from your podcast. It is the reason why you want to funnel traffic from your podcast listeners by building your audience through your subscriber email list. Therefore, I invite listeners to check out my website on both the intro and outro. On your website, you can give away a checklist, a preview of an upcoming book, offer a free strategy session, etc.

The whole point of building your list is to be able to not only give value to your readers, but also to offer products and services otherwise known as back-end products. I offer several different services including our Book Publishing Implementation Program, One-On-One Executive Coaching, Done For You Book Publishing Service, Done For You Book Launch Marketing Service, Executive Ghostwriting for Business Owners and Executives who want to share their story, and our Done For You Podcast Production Services.

I also offer public speaking and keynotes and have a speaking area on my website. Originally, my goal as an author was to increase business with my motivational speaking services and it made a significant difference where I can now charge $3,000 on average and up to

$5,000 depending on the event. I mainly speak at college campuses, but our corporate business has also increased. Those increases have happened due to offering additional seminars that expanded from motivational seminars to leadership and publishing seminars.

Offering public speaking is a great way to expand your business and having both a book and a podcast will make all the difference in increasing your public speaking business. Your book and podcast will make you an authority in your area of expertise. I give away paperback versions of my book during seminars at leadership conferences as lead magnets in return for having audience members fill out interest forms to bring me to their campus or business. It works as I typically have at least fifteen to twenty-five leads at the end of every seminar that I receive through giving away the paperback book, which is typically the book version of the seminar.

Becoming a Book Publishing Coach in early 2016 has made me a considerable amount of revenue on the back-end and the coaching combined with my motivational speaking events enabled me to leave my job as a Special Education Teacher in June 2017. This was achieved while teaching full-time, so there is time to build a business for you and a catalog of back-end products that you can offer to your listeners.

One thing I want to make clear about coaching is that you need to decide on the niche that you want to coach in if you have not already done so. Different niches include life coaching, health and wellness, spirituality, travel, real estate, helping people relocate to a new area, or book publishing. You do not want to make your coaching too general. You want it to be specific as possible to be successful. That is why I chose book publishing as my niche because I developed a proven system that works and more importantly could use the system to help other people in their author journey.

Webinars are another great way to promote your product or service. I will freely admit that I completely screwed up my first webinar product. I created a lead page and promoted it actively in the release of Motivation 101. I was selling a three-part webinar for $49.99 (which was 50 percent off the $99.99 price point). It would address three key components from the book with the first one covering Our Greatest Opponent. It failed miserably!

What I should have done was offered a FREE webinar and then sold my coaching service on the back-end. I would have most likely made a lot more revenue with that initial webinar and it was a lesson learned. Sometimes products will sell well, and sometimes they will fail.

Another back-end product that is worth considering is creating video courses. Creating an online course is a way for you to create content and have students sign up. It does take a lot of work to set up, but it is a great opportunity to make significant passive income as once your product is uploaded then you market it and start to build your business. My goal is to create multiple smaller courses in the future including how to create your own audiobook, how to become a professional speaker, and other courses.

All you need to do is purchase an account on Vimeo.com where you can upload up to five gigs of data per week. The initial account to get started costs sixty dollars per year and their business account costs twenty dollars per month. I upgraded my account to a business account due to the growth of my Book Publishing Implementation Program.

To record the content, you can use the microphone that I recommended earlier in this book and buy video capture software. I use Debut Video Capture Software. It cost me twenty-five dollars for the license in 2017 and the instructions are easy to follow. Go to https://www.nchsoftware.com/capture/index.html to get more information about their software. To create an online course, you can create between six to ten video modules. You can create power point slides through Microsoft Office or use Open Office for each module. Once the slides are created, you can use Debut to record your narration for the module. Use the information that you create in the slides for the talking points in the modules and then expand on the information when recording the narration.

The potential with online courses is to make hundreds if not thousands of dollars a month, but it does take time. The best advice I can give is to be patient. This is a marathon, not a sprint. It is a process and it takes time.

Rome was not built in a day, and it does take patience as you slowly build your back-end offerings. Therefore, I want you to be clear on what you want to get out of having your own podcast. Think about the services you want to offer through the back-end of your podcast. Is it the opportunity to do public speaking? Is it to begin or expand your professional coaching? Do you want to create an online course? Are you wanting to grow your business to take it to the next level?

Chapter 18

Summary: Podcast 101

"The best time to plant a tree was 20 years ago. The second-best time is now." Chinese Proverb

We have covered a lot of information in this book.

One thing I want to make clear is that no one can do it entirely themselves. We all need help! I am a huge believer in having help and I hired a business coach in 2017 to help me. Hiring my coach and going through his program was the best decision I ever made. The money I invested in the program was significant, but you do get what you pay for. It was life changing when I decided to hire a coach to help me implement the framework for our services.

Best part is that the investment often is tax deductible when you hire a coach and use a publisher to get published. Check with your countries tax laws, but I was able to write off the investment of hiring my own coach on my taxes. Coaching, publishing, and podcasting costs are often tax deductible and I want to mention that again as not everyone realizes the tax benefits with having your own podcast.

Having a coach brings focus, accountability, implementation, and support to getting your podcast created. It also will help build your business quickly with a proven system that works. The hardest part about starting your podcast is the implementation process, which is the primary benefit you will get should we end up working together.

One of the most important questions that you need to ask yourself is this.

What are you willing to invest to change your life?

If you are reading this book, then you are most likely at a fork in the road. You want to make a change.

The change you want to make involves either growing your business or starting a new business. If you are a business owner, having a podcast is essential to growing your business.

I was in that same situation four years ago when I wrote, published, and marketed my first book. At that time, I was making good money teaching, but I was not making a lot of additional income. After having an epiphany in Las Vegas, I started to write my first book. Once the book was written, I realized that I needed more money to be able to pay for my first launch while waiting for the royalties to come in. Once your book is launched, it takes two months to get your first royalty check from Amazon.

I knew that I would be spending at least a couple thousand dollars with publishing and marketing my first book. Once I realized the investment that was necessary, I made the decision to ask my dad for a loan. I told him my business plan and he lent me two thousand dollars, so I could get the book published and marketed properly.

That loan resulted in starting a business that now makes significant revenue four years later with multiple revenue streams on the front-end with each of my books in Kindle, audiobook, and paperback and on the back-end with speaking events, our Book Publishing Implementation Program, One-On-One Executive Coaching, Done For You Book Publishing, Done For You Book Launch Marketing Services, Executive Ghostwriting, and Done For You Podcast Production Services.

Taking that risk four years ago enabled me to leave my job as a teacher, be my own boss, and set my own hours. The commute is now ten seconds from the living room to my home office and I love it. The best part is having the opportunity to work with others to help them change their lives.

I would love to work with you through our services and especially through our Done For You Podcast Production Service.

Now it is time for you to decide and answer the following question one more time.

What are you willing to invest to change your life?

Please spread the word about our services if you know of others who are looking to change their lives. I also ask that you please pass this book on to your friends and family, so they can also benefit from the information. If there is anything I can do for you then please let me know.

On the next page, you have an invitation to set up a strategy session with me. The call is NOT a sales presentation. My intention with these calls are only to answer any questions that you have.

Thank you for investing your time in reading my book. I look forward to speaking with you and helping in your author journey to get published.

Go to GetPublishedSystem.com to find out more about our services and how you can set up a quick strategy session

Strategy Session Invitation

Are you ready to set up a complimentary strategy session?

Are you ready to grow your business with a proven system that works?

The only question we ask in our no-pitch session is "tell me how we can help." This is not a sales call. Our only intention is to see if and how we can help you.

Due to time constraints, the call must be limited to 15-minutes.

Are you ready to get started?

Go to GetPublishedSystem.com to find out more about our services and how you can set up a quick strategy session

More Books by Paul

"Quick and inexpensive reads for self-improvement, a healthier lifestyle, and book publishing"

Thirteen-time Amazon bestselling author, Paul Brodie believes that books should be inexpensive, straightforward, direct, and not have a bunch of fluff.

Each of his books were created to solve problems including living a healthy lifestyle, increasing motivation, improving positive thinking, traveling to amazing destinations, starting a podcast, and helping authors write, publish and market their books to a #1 bestseller.

What makes Paul's books different is his ability to explain complex ideas and strategies in a simple, accessible way that you can implement immediately.

Want to know more?

Go to GetPublishedSystem.com to check out Paul's eBooks (also available in paperback and audiobook format)

About the Author

Paul Brodie is the CEO of Brodie Consulting Group, which specializes in book publishing and coaching clients on how to write, publish, and market their books. He is also the President of BrodieEDU, an education consulting firm that specializes in giving motivational, business, publishing, and leadership seminars for universities and corporations.

Brodie left teaching in June 2017 after serving as an educator in multiple roles since 2008. He served as a Special Education Teacher from 2014-2017 in the Hurst-Euless-Bedford ISD (2014-2016) and Fort Worth ISD (2016-2017) while working specifically with special needs children who had Autism. In 2014-2015 he also served as the head tennis coach and lead the school to a district championship and an undefeated season.

From 2011-2014, Brodie served as a Grant Coordinator for the ASPIRE program in the Birdville Independent School District. As coordinator, he created instructional and enrichment programming for over 800 students and 100 parents in the ASPIRE before and after school programs. He also served on the Board of Directors for the Leadership Development Council, Inc. from 2005-2014 with leading the implementation of educational programming in low cost housing.

From 2008-2011, he was a highly successful teacher in Arlington, TX where he taught English as a Second Language. Brodie turned a once struggling ESL program into one of the top programs in the school district. Many of his students moved on to journalism, AVID, art classes, and many students exited the ESL program entirely.

Teaching methods during his career as an educator included daily writing practice, flash cards, picture cards, academic relays, music, movies, and short educational videos including the alphabet and sight words. Additional strategies included graphic novels paired with movie versions of the novels, games, cultural celebrations, and getting parents involved in their children's education. Brodie's approach has been called unconventional but very effective, revolutionary, and highly engaging. His students have always shown great improvement with both academics and behavior throughout the school year and he was honored to teach such an amazing and diverse group of students during his career as an educator.

Previously, Brodie spent many years in the corporate world and decided to leave a lucrative career in the medical field to follow his passion and transitioned into education. Prior to working in the medical field, he worked for Enterprise Rent-A-Car after receiving his Bachelor's Degree and for Savitz Research during his high school and college years. He is very grateful for every career opportunity as each one was an avenue to learn and grow.

Brodie earned an M.A. in Teaching from Louisiana College and B.B.A. in Management from the University of Texas at Arlington. Brodie is a bestselling author and has written multiple books. He wrote his first book, Eat Less and Move More: My Journey in the summer of 2015. Brodie's goal of the book was to help those like himself who had challenges with weight. The goal of his first book was to promote not only weight loss but also health and wellness. He is also the author of Motivation 101, Positivity Attracts, Book Publishing for Beginners, The Pursuit of Happiness, Maui (two Maui books), Just Do It, PMA, San Diego, Book Publishing for Authors, Champion, and Get Published. All thirteen books (available in Kindle, Paperback, and Audiobook) are Amazon bestsellers and are based on his motivational seminars, book publishing, love of travel, and struggles with weight.

His seminars have been featured at many universities and at leadership conferences across the United States since 2005. Brodie is active in professional organizations and within the community and currently serves on the Board of Directors for Timeless Concerts and as a volunteer with the Special Olympics. Paul is a proud Rotarian and is a member of the Arlington Chamber of Commerce and Young Men for Arlington. He continues to be involved with The International Business Fraternity of Delta Sigma Pi and has served in many positions since 2002 including National Vice President – Organizational Development, Leadership Foundation Trustee, National Organizational Development Chair, District Director, and in many other volunteer leadership roles. He resides in Arlington, TX.

Acknowledgments

Thank you to God for guidance and protection throughout my life.

Thank YOU, the reader, for investing your time reading this book.

Thank you to my amazing mom, Barbara Brodie for all the years of support and a kick in the butt when needed.

Thank you to Billy Atwell a writing great foreword for this book.

Thank you to my awesome sister, Dr. Heather Ottaway for all the help and feedback with my books and with my motivational seminars. It is scary how similar we are.

Thank you to Devin Mooneyham for serving as the editor of my book. The slicing and dicing as always was very much appreciated and I could not have gotten this book published without her assistance.

Thank you to all who have served on our Advisory Board.

Thank you to my dad, Bill "The Wild Scotsman" Brodie for his encouragement and support with the business aspects of Brodie Consulting Group.

Thank you to Shannon and Robert Winckel (two members of the four horsemen with myself and our good friend, Derrada Rubell-Asbell) for their friendship and support. Shannon and Robert are two of my best teacher friends and are always great sounding boards for ideas.

Thank you to all the amazing friends that I have worked with over the past twenty plus years. Each of them has made a great impact on my life.

Thank you to all my students that I have had the honor to teach over the years. I am very proud of each of my kids.

Thank you to Delta Sigma Pi Business Fraternity. I learned a great deal about public speaking and leadership through the organization and every experience that I have had helped me become the person that I am today.

Thank you to my three best friends: J. Dean Craig, Jen Mamber, and Aaron Krzycki. We have gone through a lot together and I look forward to many more years of friendship.

Thank you to all the students past and present at the UT Arlington and UT Austin chapters of DSP. Both schools mean a lot to me and I look forward to seeing them again at some point soon.

Thank you to the Lott Family (Stacy, Kerry, Lexi, and Austin) for their friendship over the past eight years.

Thank you to Robin Clites for always taking care of things at the house with ensuring that Mom and I can always get that family vacation every year.

Contact Information

Go to our website at
www.BrodieConsultingGroup.com and click on
the speaking and keynotes tab to see why you
should consider bringing Paul to your campus
or organization.

Paul can be reached at
Brodie@BrodieConsultingGroup.com

Website - www.GetPublishedSystem.com

Publishing and Coaching Services
www.GetPublishedSystem.com

Get Published Podcast
www.GetPublishedPodcast.com

Join our Get Published Facebook Group

Follow Paul on Instagram

Follow Paul on Twitter @Get__Published

Like Paul's Author Page on Facebook

Feedback Request

Please leave a review for my book as I would greatly appreciate your feedback.

If for some reason you did not enjoy the book then please contact me at

 Brodie@BrodieConsultingGroup.com to discuss options prior to leaving a negative review and please feel free to let me know how the book can be improved.

Made in the USA
San Bernardino, CA
06 September 2019